"This is not just another study on prayer. It is an invitation to join a Conversation—one many believers have been feeling left out of for far too long. Cynthia's transparency, biblical insight, and encouragement will help anyone who applies these principles experience a whole new level and quality of relationship with their heavenly Father/Friend."

—ARLYN LAWRENCE, coauthor of *Prayer-Saturated Kids*; editor of *PrayKids! Teacher's Guide: A Hands-On Guide for Developing Kids Who Pray*

"We need help to know how to pray, and here's a guide that can give us just that! This easy and wonderful book with practical suggestions will help us learn how to talk with God. I'm so very grateful for this much-needed resource. You will be too!"

—STEPHEN W. SMITH, founder, Potter's Inn; author of *The Lazarus Life* and *Soul Custody*

"As a prayer leader, I am often invited to review and recommend new books on prayer. However, when I read *Prayer Begins with Relationship*, I realized I did not want to recommend it to you as a book to read—instead, I highly recommend that you journey it and invite others to travel with you. *Prayer Begins with Relationship* is not meant to merely be read word after word, beginning to end. Interruptions and pauses are required! Cynthia offers us a learning experience best achieved in, no surprise, relationship—in relationship with God and also with others seeking to deepen their relationships with Him. The combination of Cynthia's insights and the tasks of study, discussion, and actual praying make this a new and useful tool for people hungry for the taste of real-life prayer."

—PHIL MIGLIORATTI, community manager, Pray! Network; founder, National Pastors' Prayer Network

PRAYER BEGINS WITH RELATIONSHIP

BREAKTHROUGH PRAYER: STUDIES FOR SMALL GROUPS

CYNTHIA HYLE BEZEK

NAVPRESS

Discipleship Inside Out®

NAVPRESS

Discipleship Inside Out®

NavPress is the publishing ministry of The Navigators, an international Christian organization and leader in personal spiritual development. NavPress is committed to helping people grow spiritually and enjoy lives of meaning and hope through personal and group resources that are biblically rooted, culturally relevant, and highly practical.

For a free catalog go to www.NavPress.com
or call 1.800.366.7788 in the United States or 1.800.839.4769 in Canada.

ISBN-13: 978-1-61521-976-6

Cover design by Arvid Wallen
Cover photo by MaxPhoto/Shutterstock

Some of the anecdotal illustrations in this book are true to life and are included with the permission of the persons involved. All other illustrations are composites of real situations, and any resemblance to people living or dead is coincidental.

Unless otherwise identified, all Scripture quotations in this publication are taken from the *Holy Bible, New International Version®* (NIV®). Copyright © 1973, 1978, 1984 by International Bible Society. Used by permission of Zondervan. All rights reserved. Other versions used include: the *Holy Bible*, New Living Translation (NLT), copyright © 1996, 2004. Used by permission of Tyndale House Publishers, Inc., Wheaton, Illinois 60189. All rights reserved; and the New King James Version (NKJV). Copyright © 1982 by Thomas Nelson, Inc. Used by permission. All rights reserved.

Printed in the United States of America

2 3 4 5 6 7 8 9 10 / 17 16 15 14 13 12

Pray!®

Deepening Your
Relationship with God
Through Prayer

Pray! resources from NavPress are for people who believe that talking with God was meant to be more than a predictable, duty-driven, one-way monologue. They're for people who want to pray with engagement, relationship, and *life*. They're for those of us who want to *experience* God and not just talk at Him.

If you're ready to break through obligation, guilt, boredom, and frustration into the relationship with God you've always wanted, *Pray!* books and resources are here to help.

Talking with God can be the satisfying connection your soul longs for. Are you ready to go deeper through prayer?

CONTENTS

INTRODUCTION

PRAYER DID NOT COME naturally for me, and my efforts at it often left me feeling frustrated and inadequate. Even now I don't consider myself a prayer giant by any means.

Then why is she writing a small-group study on prayer? you might wonder.

I'm writing because my struggles in prayer are more typical than not among believers. However, few of us like to talk about our disappointing experiences. We're embarrassed that we don't enjoy praying and don't do it more. We wish prayer were a "want to," but it's a "supposed to." However, now I truly do enjoy talking with God—a lot! Talking with Him is engaging, meaningful, even fun.

I think the reason God lets me share about prayer with you is because I can be an empathetic friend who understands the struggles. But I can also tell you that the "more" you've been wanting in prayer is possible. And it doesn't come through reading more books, trying harder, or being more disciplined; it comes through understanding what prayer really is—and knowing who God really is.

God has given me many breakthroughs during this ongoing prayer journey He and I have been on. But the single most important discovery—the realization that has changed my prayers forever—is that prayer is relationship. Prayer is inherently a relational interaction between you and God. It's a dynamic conversation between two individuals who love, care for, and enjoy one another.

The premise that prayer begins with relationship is the core idea we'll be unpacking and practicing in this study. As we do, I hope nearly everything about prayer will start changing for you: your attitudes, expectations, and emotions; the topics you bring up; the length and frequency of your prayers. And, most important, I hope you will pray because you *want* to.

HOW TO GET THE MOST FROM THIS STUDY

THIS STUDY IS DESIGNED to provide practical, hands-on opportunities for you to grow deeper in your relationship with God through prayer. With that in mind, realize that you will get the most out of the study if you do each lesson on your own and come to your group time prepared to share what you have experienced and where you may be struggling.

As a guideline, plan to spend twenty to thirty minutes a day in the lesson. You will be asked to read Scripture, reflect, respond, and try out what you learn in prayer practice.

How you divide up the lessons over a week's time is up to you. I'll give suggestions for how you can proportion your time, but feel free to work through them in the manner that works best for you. The most important thing is to pace yourself so you allow several days for the prayer portions.

As you work through the questions that open each lesson, please don't approach them with the goal of looking up verses to find the "right" answer to a question. This is not a fill-in-the-blank study where you "succeed" if you learn more information. Rather, the questions will help you think, reflect, and feel in ways that will spur you into a deeper connection with God. You will probably respond to questions differently from other people in your group—this is good! Be yourself and enjoy the variety exhibited among members of your group.

Because the object of this study is not to learn *about* prayer but actually *to pray*—and through prayer to deepen your relationship with God—the prayer part is essential. If you work through the interactive questions and participate in group discussion but do not practice praying, you will miss the whole point of the study. So when a portion of the lesson says to talk with God about something, please talk with God about it. You learn to pray by praying.

Each lesson has the same three elements: (1) "Consider This," which includes interactive questions to introduce the lesson's key idea; (2) a section called "Talk It Over," where you'll find prayer exercises that will help you talk with God; and (3) "Continue to Practice," where I'll give you one or more ideas for how to build this key idea into your daily life with God.

At the beginning of each lesson, I'll include a suggestion of how you might split up the lesson over a week, but it's only that: a suggestion. There isn't a right or wrong way here. Work through the questions and prayer responses at a pace that works for you; just be sure to *pray*.

This study will probably be different from other studies you have done. Many studies are aimed at gaining information about the Bible or a spiritual topic. This one aims to transform how you relate with God. And learning information won't do that. Real change will happen if you are willing to adopt several important approaches:

- Be honest with yourself and God about where you are in your relationship with Him and how you feel about talking with Him. Prayer is a vulnerable topic for many people, even pastors and spiritual leaders. Many of us (maybe even most of us) are not where we want to be when it comes to prayer. If you are willing to be honest about your disappointments and struggles, this study can move you closer to where you hope to be.

- Be willing to be stretched. Some of the questions and exercises will move you out of your comfort zone. Please enter in, even if you are doubtful or unsure. Others who have done this study reported that if they were willing to try the prayer responses, they were surprised at how God met them and how talking with God became more rewarding.

• Respect where you are—and where others in your group are—on your journey with God in prayer. Don't be afraid to share your struggles and disappointments with other members. At the same time, be sensitive when other members share their weaknesses. Don't try to coach them with what works for you. Let the Holy Spirit do that. Accept others where they are right now. Help create a safe environment for everyone to be vulnerable.

Note to Group Leaders: A leader's guide can be downloaded at www.navpress.com (search for *Prayer Begins with Relationship*). You'll find detailed information in the guide for how to begin and facilitate this study.

A FRIEND OF GOD

KEY IDEA:

Prayer is inherently relational; it thrives in the context of an authentic, dynamic, reciprocating friendship with God.

> **SUGGESTIONS FOR PACING THE LESSON**
>
> Days 1–2: Work through the questions in the "Consider This" section and do the first prayer response under "Talk It Over."
>
> Days 3–7: Do the second prayer response and complete the "Continue to Practice" suggestions.

FOR YEARS I WORKED fairly diligently at two aspects of my spiritual life: my relationship with God and prayer.

I wanted to be close to God and thought that doing the "right things" — studying my Bible, having a quiet time, committing to my church, using my spiritual gifts, serving God — would automatically bring loving closeness with Him. But it didn't. So I kept doing the only thing I knew to do: I kept working — and hoping one day I'd figure it out.

I also worked hard at prayer. God wanted it — He even commanded it — yet I found prayer difficult and often tedious. Somehow I needed to learn to pray! I read books on prayer, kept prayer lists and journals, went to prayer meetings, and basically followed any prayer opportunity that presented itself. For a long time I remained disappointed, and then I heaped guilt onto myself because I just couldn't get it even though I was trying so hard.

One day God showed me something that forever changed my approach to both prayer and relationship with Him. It was very simple but incredibly profound: *Prayer begins with relationship.* The key to both vital prayer and vital relationship with God is found in learning to communicate with Him in the context of loving relationship. That breakthrough, more than anything else, set me on a new and exciting course of knowing God, enjoying Him, and connecting in conversation with Him.

CONSIDER THIS

1. You've likely heard Christians talk about having a "personal relationship with God." They may explain that while other people follow a religion, they have a relationship. Consider what you think it means to have a personal relationship with God.

a. What makes it personal?

b. What makes it a relationship?

When I think of a personal relationship, I think of a unique connection between two people who know one another from firsthand experience. I think of friends or relatives who have a close bond, who interact, talk, and share life with one another. So to me, if my relationship with God is really to be "personal," then it must include the interaction, communication, and sharing of life that nurture a close bond between Him and me.

2. Most Christians agree that the primary reason God created people was to enjoy relating with them, but we might not always enter the full range of relationship He invites us into. He has given us many pictures and descriptions of how He relates with us: High Priest and worshippers, Shepherd and sheep, Vine and branches, Hen and chicks, Judge and defendants, Creator and creation, Ruler and subjects, Bridegroom and bride, Master and servants, Teacher and students — just to name a few. Many of us limit ourselves to one or two of these relational aspects, often "Ruler and subjects" or "Master and servants." In this study, we will focus on a relationship mode that sets a key foundation to prayer: Friend and friends.

It's important to know that by emphasizing friendship with God, I am not dismissing or downplaying His other roles. All aspects of God's character are important. We want to know Him and relate to Him in all of who He is. However, because many of us do not often relate to Him as Friend, that is where we will focus in this study.[1] If we will risk entering into that friendship, it promises to bring incredible life, freedom, excitement, and enjoyment to prayer.

There are many different aspects to any friendship. Among these are:

- Doing things together
- Asking for advice and input
- Giving gifts
- Covering each other's backs
- Enjoying each other
- Trusting each other
- Challenging and debating

1. The next study in this series will explore how we can pray according to the other ways God relates to us, including Shepherd, Creator, Savior, and King.

- Sharing secrets
- Laughing together
- Caring for one another's children and grandchildren
- Pleasing each other
- Offering hospitality
- Doing favors
- Sharing conversation

Consider what a friendship with God might be like.

a. What aspects from the list can you imagine it including? Circle those.

b. Which aspects of friendship seem harder to imagine as possibilities for friendship with God? Put a question mark next to those.

c. Jot thoughts about what you marked and why. (We'll come back to this list later.)

3. Let's look at two people in the Old Testament whose relationships with God included friendship. Both Abraham and Moses were called God's friends (see Exodus 33:11; 2 Chronicles 20:7; Isaiah 41:8; James 2:23). Read about Abraham and Moses in the following passages and note aspects of a Friend-to-friend relationship that you see (it may help to refer to the list of friendship characteristics in question 2).

a. Abraham, Genesis 18

b. Moses, Exodus 33:7-17

4. God also entered into friendships with people in the New Testament. Read John 15:9-17. Jesus vulnerably shared His life with the men and women He lived among. They rightly viewed Him as Teacher and Master. But Jesus wanted more than students and servants. He said, "I no longer call you servants. . . . Instead, I have called you friends" (verse 15). Jesus wasn't saying He would no longer be their teacher or master; He was adding friendship to the ways they would relate with Him.

a. How is the relationship between a master and a servant different from the relationship between friends? On the next page, brainstorm the characteristics of each relationship.

Master and servant   **Friend and friend**

b. Put yourself in the place of one of the twelve disciples who has been with Jesus daily for the past three years. You eagerly accepted His teaching, looked to Him for direction each morning when you got up, and anticipated the day He would be your political leader. How might you have responded when Jesus announced that He wanted to change the way you related to Him and was now going to call you His friend? Would you feel eager? Intimidated? Offended? Honored? Would you want to relate to Him as a friend, or would you want to remain in only the servant role? Why?

5. "But I'm not Moses or Abraham or even one of the disciples," you may be saying. "Surely you're not saying God would want *me* for a friend!"

The Bible seems to suggest exactly that! On the same evening Jesus announced His desire to relate to the disciples as friends, He prayed a prayer for all believers, including those who would believe because of the disciples' testimony—in other words, you. Read John 17:20-26, which picks up in the middle of Jesus' prayer.

a. What two things does Jesus want for all who believe in Him (verse 21)?

b. What does He want people to know about the level of love the Father has for those who believe in His Son (verse 23)?

c. What degree of closeness does Jesus want those who believe in Him to have with Him (verse 24)?

d. Does the relationship Jesus describes and asks for with all of His followers—present and future—sound more like a Master/servant relationship or a Friend/friend relationship? Why?

I first gave the idea of friendship with God serious thought when my life took a hard left turn during my midthirties. My husband, son, and I had moved 1,000 miles across the country, leaving behind family and friends we'd known all our lives. Within our first year in that new city, my husband was diagnosed with multiple sclerosis. We'd been in our new church only a few months and hardly knew anyone. The very few people I did know couldn't understand what I was feeling, even though they tried. This was the worst loneliness I'd ever experienced. I needed a best friend. I'd heard that God was supposed to be that kind of friend, but I had no idea how to connect with Him.

Of course I prayed—a lot. I asked God to heal my husband. I pleaded for wisdom for the many medical decisions we needed to make. I requested strength and endurance. I apologized to Him for being afraid (my fear felt like an affront to His sovereignty). But I didn't relate to Him as a close friend. I didn't pour out my confusion and hurt. I didn't just sit with Him and cry. I didn't ask Him to keep me company during the darkest times. And I also didn't experience much of His understanding, compassion, or comfort. I didn't know such a connection was even possible. Consequently, I continued feeling incredibly alone, and, to be frank, I was disappointed that God didn't seem to be there for me.

I'm thankful that's not the end of my story. In the years since then, God has opened up a more intimate relationship with Him than I ever imagined possible—a relationship that came primarily through prayer. But He had to enlarge my understanding of prayer in order to do so. You see, even though I knew that prayer included worship, confession, and asking God to do things, I didn't know that prayer also meant personal interaction—communication.

6. Look back at the list of aspects found in friendship (see pages 17–18). Which ones require communication?

You probably see what I'm driving at. Simply put, God invites us to be His friends, and meaningful friendship requires good communication. It follows, then, that friendship with God involves conversation. Give-and-take with each other. Sharing. Listening. Responding.

If communication is the key to successful relationships between husbands and wives, parents and children, bosses and employees, and friends, doesn't it stand to reason that our most important relationship—our relationship with God—would have loving, effective communication at its core?

7.   What I've just said may have raised a variety of thoughts, feelings, and questions for you. Jot them in the space provided. In future lessons, we'll start unpacking this foundational idea.

TALK IT OVER

As I mentioned, this course isn't a traditional study where mere learning is the goal. The questions you've just completed are designed to prepare you for the focal point of each lesson: prayer itself.

After each lesson's "Consider This" section, I'll give you ways to talk with God in the "Talk It Over" section. As you talk with Him in these responses, ask Him to work what you're learning into your life so it becomes an agent of transformation. You might do that by praying a simple prayer along these lines: "God, I don't just want to learn facts about You and about prayer; I want vital communication with You that is based on loving relationship, so please engage with me now."

Do the first prayer response today and try the second one tomorrow.

PRAYER RESPONSE 1: "IF WE'RE TALKING AS FRIENDS . . ."

1. Write down something you are praying about. It doesn't have to be a major life issue—just anything you happen to be praying about right now.

2. In question 4, you identified characteristics of a Master-and-servant relationship and a Friend-to-friend relationship. Your answers there, and in the following questions, can help you reflect on how your relationship with God affects the way you talk with Him about the prayer topic you just wrote down.

a. How would you pray about this topic if you thought of God as only your Master?

b. How would you pray about this if you also thought of God as your Friend?

c. What kind of response might you hope for from God in each case?

Master   **Friend**

3. Keeping in mind what you wrote under "Friend," talk with God now, friend to Friend, about what's on your mind and heart. Summarize your conversation here.

PRAYER RESPONSE 2: TALK ABOUT FRIENDSHIP

1. Take a few minutes to talk to God about your relationship with Him by choosing one of the following questions to ask Him:

- "How do You view our relationship right now, God?"
- "God, to be honest, I'm more comfortable calling You 'Master' than 'Friend.' Would You help me understand where my hesitation comes from?"
- "What would make my friendship with You even more pleasurable for You, God?"
- "When I look at the list on pages 17–18 about the elements of friendship, these are the ones I'd really like to share with You: _____. Which ones would You like to share with me?"
- "I wish I could experience more of Your friendship, God. Would You show me anything that hinders us from having the closeness we both want?"

2. Pray the question in your own words, and then wait silently for God's response. One common way He speaks to us is through our own thoughts. Record any thoughts you have that might be Him. Or, if you prefer, answer the question according to what you think He might say. Summarize your conversation here.

FRIENDSHIP WITH GOD

Relating to God as friend is a tough concept for some of us. It might even seem irreverent or arrogant. After all, how can we be friends with the King of kings, Creator of the universe, a holy and sinless God? Keep the following points in mind as you try to wrap your mind and heart around Jesus' incredible invitation.

- Our friendship with God is not a friendship of equals. He will always remain in His rightful place of honor and authority. We are still the work of His hands, His people over whom He has final say. That never changes, no matter how close or intimate we become with Him. In fact, according to Psalm 25:14 a proper respect of God is part of being His friend: "The Lord is a friend to those who fear him" (NLT).

- God has a very high view of friendship. To Him, friendship means being willing to lay down your life for the one you love (see John 15:13). This is the kind of friendship He calls us to, not a disposable, easy-come-easy-go friendship between "pals." Relating to Him as a friend may even bring greater depth and meaning to your human relationships as you learn about friendship from Him.

- Friendship is just one of the ways God relates with us. God is many things to us at the same time, including Father, Shepherd, Lord, Redeemer, Teacher, and Friend. No one aspect of who He is cancels out the rest. The better we know Him — in all of His various aspects — the more accurately we'll be able to relate to Him, talk with Him, and enjoy Him.

- Friendship with God is not only for our benefit. He is a Person with feelings. Consider what it means that we, who all want friends, are created in God's image: He wants friends too. Not many people are willing to go there. But those who take Him seriously and enter into that deep relationship with Him bring Him great joy.

CONTINUE TO PRACTICE

For the remaining days this week, ask God each morning to show you where He'd like you to be a friend to Him today. Then keep your spiritual eyes and ears open! Pay attention to:

- Things that go better than you anticipated. These might be your Friend lending you a helping hand or offering encouragement. Thank Him!
- Situations you'd usually handle on your own. Invite your Friend into them and ask for His input.
- Nudges to connect or pray with someone. This might be God asking you to care about someone who is on His heart.
- Times when you feel alone. Pray something like this: "Thank You for being my Friend. Help me to feel Your presence." Pray it slowly and repeat it as often as necessary until you start to sense His presence.
- Times of enjoyment. Notice what you enjoy — nature, a song on the radio, the face of a child or a friend, a joke, art, a stunning sports play. Talk to God and ask Him to enjoy the moment with you, as you would with a friend.

Record your experiences of these moments of friendship with God.

Notes About Your Experience:

THE RISK OF BEING REAL

KEY IDEA:
Our friendship with God deepens when we risk being open and honest as we talk with Him.

MY HUSBAND SPENT ALMOST six years in a wheelchair before he died of multiple sclerosis. His impossible-to-ignore condition drew the attention of lots of well-meaning people, and I genuinely appreciated their concern. However, I was taken aback by the number of people—some whom I didn't even know—who expected me to open up and be vulnerable with them. They'd try to draw me out by saying, "This must be so hard for you. How do you deal with all the loss you're facing?" Many would add, "If you ever need to talk, please give me a call." They'd even urge, "Call anytime, day or night." I knew they were trying to be compassionate, and I desperately needed to get real with someone. But becoming vulnerable with people I barely knew was more than I dared to do.

Before I'd risk spilling my guts, I needed an idea of how people would respond. I needed to know I would be safe and accepted. I

> **SUGGESTIONS FOR PACING THE LESSON**
>
> Days 1-3: Work through the questions and begin the prayer responses.
>
> Days 4-7: Continue with the prayer responses and begin the practice prayers.

needed assurance that I'd receive understanding, compassion, hope, and encouragement. I definitely did not want advice, pat answers, or Christian exhortations that would burden me even more. Because vulnerability posed such a huge risk, I'd shift the conversations to small talk whenever possible.

CONSIDER THIS

1. Your experiences are different from mine, but can you relate to any part of my story? If so, describe a time when you were hesitant to say what you really thought, felt, needed, or longed for.

Eventually God gave me some men and women with whom it felt safe to open up. I talked about my questions and feelings — including ones that didn't seem very "Christian" to me, such as anger, doubt, impatience, and resentment. Our conversations were comforting and, in the end, healing and strengthening. The friendships that emerged from those times of gut-honest sharing have been deep and enduring.

I've been describing a common dilemma: It's hard to be vulnerable with someone unless you're in close relationship. Yet it's hard for a relationship to become close if you're not vulnerable. So, somehow, if we want relationships that go past the surface, we're going to have to risk opening up.

The same is true when we relate to God. Last week we learned that prayer is relational and that it thrives in the context of an authentic friendship with God. This week we will explore the truth that your friendship with God deepens when you risk being open and honest as you talk with Him—when you bring your real self to Him in prayer.

Though some of us don't like the idea, being open and honest involves sharing feelings. It was one thing for me to tell a friend, "Taking care of my husband yesterday was really hard." But our friendship had a chance to grow when I trusted my friend enough to say, "Taking care of my husband yesterday was really hard. I kept thinking that he was the one who was supposed to protect and provide for me, not the other way around. I hate feeling this way, but sometimes I am overwhelmed by fear and self-pity."

2. Jesus lived openly with those around Him. He permitted Himself to express a full range of emotions, including positive ones such as joy, love, and compassion and emotions many of us would consider negative, such as anger, indignation, and impatience. Read the following Bible passages and note what Jesus felt and the emotions He displayed.

   a. Matthew 26:36-46

   b. Mark 3:1-6

   c. Mark 10:13-16

   d. Mark 10:17-22

e. Luke 7:11-15

f. Luke 10:17-24

g. Luke 19:41-44

h. John 2:12-17

i. John 11:32-44

3. Which story stood out to you or stirred a reaction in you? Choose a person in that story (other than Jesus) and imagine yourself in his or her place. How does Jesus' emotional honesty and vulnerability affect you? How would you respond to Him?

4. Jesus didn't ignore His emotions or keep them hidden from others. Rather, He shared Himself fully and honestly. So it seems that if we're going to do life with Him, we'd better get used to His emotional openness. We should probably also consider that He wants us to engage fully with Him too—mind and heart, thoughts and emotions.

Yet opening up to Jesus isn't always easy. We probably feel free to tell Him about our joys, but in real life we also struggle with sin, injustice, pain, and temptation. These situations arouse feelings that are not comfortable. It seems riskier to be honest when we feel isolated, guilty, irritated, intimidated, ashamed, angry, inadequate, rejected, or worthless.

Part of the reason for our hesitation is that many of us have tried to open up only to face a negative response. Perhaps the other person brushed us off or chided us or gave us a pat answer seasoned with happy talk. Anyone who's had an experience like that is probably not eager to try it again. But just because people have reacted to us that way, does that mean our compassionate, wise, and perfect Friend will also react that way?

Since Jesus experienced emotions, including negative ones, how do you think He feels toward you when you are experiencing painful or uncomfortable emotions? Is this different from how you feel about yourself when you experience a negative emotion? If so, how?

5. The fact that Jesus knows us fully and became human in every way offers rich benefits for our honest conversations with Him. Read about Jesus in Hebrews 2:17-18 and 4:14-16. What are some of these benefits? Which mean the most to you?

God showed me how much He cares about my feelings a few months ago when my computer died—for the third time in two years. I lost everything: projects for work, my prayer journal from the previous five years, my address book. But unlike the previous crashes, this time the guy who helps me with my computer said there was no hope of recovering what I'd lost. Worse, I didn't have backups. After the previous disasters, I knew I should back up my files, but I'd never done it.

So I stuffed down my disappointment and moved on to the massive job of redoing my work. What else could I do?

A few weeks later a friend in my Bible study asked the group to pray about his crashed computer. Like mine, his situation seemed hopeless. While he was talking, I sheepishly realized I hadn't even thought to talk to God about my computer. A little timidly, I asked the group to pray for my files, too. But then I didn't think any more about it.

Two days later a friend asked me to pray about computer issues that were preventing her from carrying out ministry. Obviously, a theme was emerging. I prayed for her technical difficulties and also took her prayer request as a gentle reminder from the Lord. It seemed He really wanted me to ask Him to restore my lost files.

"I think I finally hear You," I prayed. "Okay then, will You please help?"

Almost immediately I sensed Him speaking in my heart: "How do you feel about your lost files?"

"How do I feel about them? What does it matter how I feel?"

He just repeated the question.

Suddenly it hit me. I felt embarrassed, irresponsible, and stupid. I knew I should have backed up my files, but I didn't do it. I didn't know how to do a backup, and I didn't think I was smart enough to learn. The loss was my fault, and I didn't deserve help. That's why I didn't want to talk to God about my computer problems—because of those emotions and beliefs I'd stuffed down and thought I had to keep to myself.

Because God seemed to already know about (and care about) how I felt, I risked going ahead and telling Him. "I feel stupid and irresponsible, God. This is all my fault. I have only myself to blame. This is just the price for my irresponsibility. I don't deserve Your help."

I sensed His deep compassion as He said, "I do not treat you like that! I long to redeem your mistakes. I want to help those who cannot help themselves. I am full of mercy and compassion, and I want to rescue you. Will you let Me?"

Less than a day later, a friend asked if I'd like him to look at my computer and see if God would help him find my files. Long story short, God did it! He restored the files I'd lost. I was overjoyed to get all of my work and files back, but even more to realize how trustworthy He was to receive me—just like a good friend—when I risked opening up about what was really going on.[2]

6. God worked on two levels in the story you just read. Why do you think He wasn't content to meet only my practical need but also wanted to talk about how I felt?

---

2. And yes, now I back up my computer.

7. If you really thought God would offer personalized understanding and compassion if you risked sharing honest feelings with Him, how would your prayer life change? How would your relationship with Him change?

TALK IT OVER

TALKING POINTS

As you talk with God, remember to practice the key ideas we've focused on last week and this week:

1. Prayer is relational, so talk to God as you would to a friend.

2. Risk talking openly and honestly about what you feel and think.

Choose one of the following prayer prompts and use it to help you talk with God about the ideas in the questions you just completed. (Obviously, you can do more than one if you'd like.)

PRAYER RESPONSE 1: "I'M JUST NOT EMOTIONAL"

Some of us don't think we're particularly emotional, or we might not believe emotions are important. (Although we more often think of men as being nonemotional, many women also are unaware of their feelings or reluctant to admit them.)

1. If "I'm just not emotional" describes you, talk to Jesus about your viewpoint. Select at least two of the questions below to begin a conversation with Him.

    ☐ "Jesus, I'm surprised that You were so open with Your feelings. Could You talk to me about that?"

    ☐ "I don't understand why it's important for me to acknowledge and express emotions. Would You give me Your perspective on that?"

    ☐ "Jesus, I wonder if I'm missing anything by ignoring my emotional side. What do You think?"

    ☐ "How would my relationship with You and with people be different if I were to live more from my heart, Jesus?"

    ☐ "Jesus, I don't really *want* to be more emotional because _____. What do You think or feel about that?"

2. Ask Jesus your questions, and then sit silently for a bit. Expect Him to speak to your spirit—perhaps with a thought, word, scripture, memory, picture, or even a feeling. Record what you sense Him saying to you.

3. Respond to Jesus. In this manner, keep the conversation going until it seems like both you and Jesus have expressed your honest thoughts and feelings. Summarize your conversation here.

PRAYER RESPONSE 2: "TO BE HONEST, I FEEL . . ."

What emotions are you carrying inside? They might be related to something major, such as a relationship in crisis, or to something more everyday, such as your inability to get along with that guy who works next to you. Or perhaps your emotions don't come from a situation. Maybe you have a dream or longing you haven't dared talk about for fear someone might discourage you or make fun of you.

Will you risk talking to Jesus? You might start by saying something like, "Jesus, I really don't want to tell You this, but I guess You already know it: I feel pretty inadequate when it comes to _____, so I've been avoiding _____ . . ." Or you might say, "Jesus, I don't think I've ever told You this before because I've been a bit afraid You'd say it wasn't spiritual enough, but I have a real longing for _____ . . ."

For the purposes of this conversation, avoid asking for answers and solutions. Focus on being as honest as possible about your concern. Try not to hide anything from Him — even if it means talking about things that embarrass, worry, anger, or depress you.

COMMON NEGATIVE **EMOTIONS**

Sometimes we need help identifying what we are feeling before we can talk to God about our emotions. Below are a few commonly felt negative emotions.

- Anxiety
- Worry
- Fear
- Dread
- Insecurity
- Shame
- Embarrassment
- Inadequacy
- Emptiness
- Rejection

- Worthlessness
- Anger
- Numbness
- Guilt
- Jealousy
- Inferiority
- Grief
- Hopelessness
- Condemnation

Write the first sentence or two of your conversation with God here.

PRAYER RESPONSE 3: "I'M NOT QUITE THERE YET"

If you're not ready to risk talking that personally with Jesus, that's okay. Instead of rushing into a conversation about emotions, talk to Him about why you hesitate.

1. Are you worried He will respond in a way that will make you feel worse? Are you concerned that He will tell you what you don't want to hear or that He won't think your issue is important? Let Him know what holds you back. If you don't know, ask Him to tell you, and then listen for His reply. Write the first sentence or two of what you tell Him.

2. Now, try to imagine Jesus responding to what you just told Him. Based on what you discovered in this lesson about how He shared His emotions with others and the ways He receives you as your High Priest, what do you think He might say or do in response to what you have just told Him? Write your impressions.

CONTINUE TO PRACTICE

Continue practicing emotional openness with God. Before you start your day, ask God to help you be aware of what you feel throughout the day. Then, toward the end of each day, talk to Him about what He has shown you. Whether you talk about a burden, joy, tension, or hope, drop your normal prayer words and tone and just talk with Him as you would a close friend. Open up. Expect Him to respond to you with compassion and understanding, and then wait in silence for His response. Make notes of your experiences.

Alternatively (or additionally, if you have time), you may wish to spend more time with the prayer responses above. Feel free to try them all or even to repeat one that you'd like to talk more about with God.

Notes About Your Experience:

UPGRADING YOUR VIEW OF GOD

KEY IDEA:

A skewed view of God shuts down our prayers, but relating to God as He actually is fosters freedom and confidence in prayer.

SUGGESTIONS FOR PACING THE LESSON

Days 1–3: Work on the "Consider This" questions and the "Talk It Over" prayer responses.

Days 4–7: Continue with the prayer responses if you'd like, and then begin to use the "Continue to Practice" prayer.

CONSIDER THIS

1. Think of a friend you've gotten to know well over time. Was there something about the person that originally puzzled or put you off but now you understand? Maybe you were a little hurt that your new friend changed the subject when you tried to tell her about the Father's Day gift you'd just bought, but now you understand she struggles with the death of her father. Maybe your friend seemed aloof, but you later realized he is just shy. How do you talk to that friend differently as a result of knowing him or her better?

Just as our perceptions or misperceptions of people affect our conversations with them, our views of God affect how we pray. Last week we discussed the importance of being open and honest with God. But who of us wants to risk bringing our true selves to God unless we're certain He will accept us and love us whatever our condition? This week, we'll see that a skewed view of God shuts down our prayers, but relating to God as He actually is fosters freedom and confidence in prayer. Upgrading our views of God to match His true character is essential if we are to develop a real relationship with Him and talk to Him freely and openly as a friend.

Like me, you probably know certain truths about God: He is love, He is faithful, He is patient and forgiving. These truths are good basic theology. However, we often have another set of beliefs about God that we hold almost subconsciously. We don't consciously *think* them, much less say them aloud. Nevertheless, these perceptions, even if they are buried deep out of sight, affect the way we relate with God. I sometimes refer to these two sets of beliefs as our "head" beliefs (what we say we believe) and our "heart" beliefs (the perceptions that actually shape our feelings and reactions to circumstances and our relationship with God).

For example, I may believe in my head that God will protect me and provide for me and not let any genuine harm come to me. But when the doctor orders a second test "just to rule out cancer" or when I face a foreclosure, that belief about God isn't the one I operate out of. Instead, a misperception about God might take over and shape my thoughts and responses, whether or not I articulate it to myself. Maybe I *really* believe "God is allowing me to suffer so I will finally grow up and develop some character" or "God is disciplining me because I've been holding out on Him."

These heart beliefs stem from a variety of sources (everything from one-sided teaching to negative experiences with significant authority figures). They generally aren't entirely wrong; they're often twisted just enough to create a barrier to approaching God as He really is in all His love and goodness.

2. Read the following perceptions of God. Are any of them similar to views you currently hold or have held? Check as many as resonate with you.

- ☐ *Enforcer.* God is always watching me to see if I'm obeying. When I mess up, I can be pretty sure of His anger, disappointment, or punishment.
- ☐ *Strong, silent type.* I know God exists, and He is powerful and good. But He's generally quiet, and I don't expect much interaction from Him.
- ☐ *High and lofty one.* God is Creator and King of the universe. He deserves the utmost honor and respect. I revere Him, but I certainly don't expect to become intimate or familiar with Him.
- ☐ *Amorphous force.* God is a spirit, kind of vague and nebulous. He's not so much a person as a cosmic force I must try to align with.
- ☐ *Never satisfied.* There's always something God seems to be nagging me about, always something He needs me to do to make Him happy. Guilt is His primary means of motivating me.
- ☐ *Indulgent.* Because He is concerned chiefly with my happiness, God won't allow much difficulty in my life. He'll give me what I ask for when I ask for it. When I get myself into trouble, He'll spare me any consequences.
- ☐ *Busy with big issues.* With the world's 6.7 billion people, wars, uprisings, earthquakes, famines, and plagues, God doesn't bother with my everyday concerns. I go to Him for the big things, but everyday matters I handle on my own.
- ☐ *Lessons to teach.* Everything that happens to me is to teach me a lesson. Pain and hardship, which God allows me to experience in generous proportions, are all about training me in godly character. I will continue to experience a particular trial until I "get" what God is trying to teach me.

☐   *Mission control.* God's primary concern is that I am busy carrying out His ministry. He relies on me to evangelize, love the poor, meet the needs of others, serve my church, and always be available for His next assignment.

☐   Other:

I used to have the perception that God was constantly monitoring my thoughts, feelings, and behavior to make sure I met His standards. I imagined Him sitting in a giant control booth in heaven surrounded by screens full of flickering lights — one of those lights represented me. If I was in trouble with God about anything, my light blinked off. That meant I had better do something to get back into His good graces and be a shining light again.

I would never have taught that view of God to anyone — or even said it out loud. I knew the Bible taught that God loved me and that my relationship with Him was based on grace not performance. But somehow all my sound theology wasn't enough to override my inaccurate perception.

Needless to say, my relationship with the Lord was greatly affected by this sad impression. I often felt as if He were upset with me and I would never be able to measure up or please Him, so my conversations with Him — if you could call them that — were formal and surfacy at best. I often avoided talking to Him altogether.

3. In the first lesson you were asked to entertain the idea that God wants to relate to you as His friend, not merely as His servant. Spend some time thinking about the views of God you identified with above.

How do these affect your ability to talk to God as your Friend? Jot your thoughts and realizations here.

4. Following are just a few of the characteristics that are true of God and that enable us to talk freely and openly with Him. Check the ones you regularly experience as you pray.

☐ Delights in and takes pleasure in me (Psalm 147:11; Zephaniah 3:17)

☐ Cares about even the smallest details of my life (Matthew 6:31-32; Luke 12:6-7)

☐ Pities (has compassion on) me when I'm hurting (Psalm 72:12-14; Isaiah 63:9; 2 Corinthians 1:3-4)

☐ Is patient with and understanding of my weaknesses and failures (Psalm 103:12-14; Hebrews 4:15-16)

☐ Wants to help me out of the messes I get myself into (Psalm 40:1-3; Isaiah 61:7)

☐ Enjoys sharing His heart with me (Psalm 25:14; Matthew 11:25-26)

☐ Likes to hear what I think and feel (Psalm 62:8; 1 Peter 5:7)

☐ Is always happy to see me, even when I've sinned against Him (Luke 15:1-2,11-24)

☐ Always has time for me (Deuteronomy 31:6; Psalm 139:7-10; Hebrews 13:5)

☐ Wants to rescue me when I'm in trouble (Psalm 91:14-15; 2 Timothy 4:18; 2 Peter 2:9)

TALK IT OVER

With a topic like the one in this lesson, it's important to relate with God about what you've uncovered. Use one of the following prayer responses today and the other tomorrow. Because upgrading your view of God can be a process, you may need to return to one or both of these prayer responses later this week—or even after this study is finished.

PRAYER RESPONSE 1: UPGRADE YOUR VIEW

1. Look again at the misconceptions you marked in the list on pages 47–48. Pick the one that resonated most strongly with you and write it here.

2. Chances are good you already know a more accurate view of God that counteracts this. Who is God *really*, in contrast to the misperception you have of Him? If you need help, review the statements and scriptures from question 4 (you could also ask for input from your group leader or a friend). Describe Him more accurately here.

3. Now share with God your thoughts and feelings about this misperception you have of Him. If it would be helpful, use one or more of the following prompts to get you started.

- "God, I think I might view You this way because . . ."
- "I think my relationship with You and my ability to talk with You would change in this way [_____] if I viewed You more accurately." (Review your answer to question 3 on page 49, if it would be helpful.)
- "I'd like to upgrade my view of You, God, but I need Your help with _____."

PRAYER RESPONSE 2: EXPERIENCE GOD AS HE IS

1. From the list in question 4, were there any characteristics you don't experience as much as you'd like?

   a. Identify up to three you would like to experience more regularly. Write them on the lines provided below.

   (1) _____

(2) _____

(3) _____

b. Look up the scriptures that go along with each. Imagine God were to personalize the words of those scriptures for you. Write down what you think that might sound like. Here's an example I did for a characteristic I'd like to experience more:

(1) *Is patient with and understanding of my weaknesses and failures (Psalm 103:12-14; Hebrews 4:15-16).*

"Cynthia, My daughter, I'm a tender and compassionate Father to you. I understand how weak you are. I made you, remember?

And Jesus, your big Brother, knows how tough it is to live in your fallen world. He experienced the same testing you do. But I have mercy and grace for you. I have removed your sins from you, as far as the east is from the west, as far as you can imagine. I don't think of you in terms of your weaknesses and failings. I think of you with love and compassion because you are Mine and I love you. Don't be afraid. Come to Me!"

c. If you really believed God felt and meant what you imagined Him saying, how would it affect you? How would it influence the way you pray? Talk to Him about this by writing your response below. If it would be helpful, use one or more of the following prompts to get you started.

- "God, it amazes me to hear You say _____ because . . ."
- "Father, I feel _____ when I hear You say these things to me, and I . . ."
- "If I were really able to believe You felt this way, it would change . . ."

CONTINUE TO PRACTICE

God says in Jeremiah 24:7, "I will give them a heart to know me, that I am the LORD." As you've seen this week, knowing God is more than just believing correct theological facts about Him. If you're to really know Him, your heart must line up with what your head believes. This is tough work to do on your own, but God wants to help. He wants to give you a heart to know Him. Turn Jeremiah 24:7 into a prayer to express your desire to have such a heart. Write your prayer here.

Use the prayer you just crafted (or a similar one) each morning to express your desire to God. Then watch and listen for the ways He will invite you to know Him more deeply and accurately. Take the risk and respond honestly to whatever He shows you. At the end of each day, talk with Him about how your view of Him is changing. If progress seems slow, talk to Him about that, too. Your main goal is to keep before you (1) your desire to know Him in truth and (2) His patient, loving desire to help you know Him as He really is.

Notes About Your Experience:

DOES GOD SPEAK? (AND AM I READY FOR THAT?)

KEY IDEA:

God is talkative and wants to engage us in two-way communication.

CONSIDER THIS

1. In lesson 1, we talked about what it means to be in a personal relationship with God. We also talked about many aspects of friendship. I described a personal relationship as "a unique connection between two people who know one another from firsthand experience, such as friends or relatives who have a close bond, who interact, talk, and share life with one another."

> **SUGGESTIONS FOR PACING THE LESSON**
>
> Days 1–3: Work through the "Consider This" questions.
>
> Days 4–7: Talk to God using the "Talk It Over" prayer response and "Continue to Practice" exercise and record your experiences.
>
> If you like, spend an optional study day with the "For Further Study" segment at the end of question 3. However, don't skimp on the prayer times in order to do this.

Among the aspects of a close friendship were:

- Doing things together
- Asking for advice and input
- Giving gifts
- Covering each other's backs
- Trusting each other
- Challenging and debating
- Pleasing each other
- Offering hospitality
- Doing favors
- Sharing conversation

a. Circle any elements of the description and any items on the list that require two-way communication.

b. Notice that there is a close connection between two-way communication and personal relationship. How are relationships affected if communication is one-sided or completely absent?

You probably see where I'm going with these questions. Like any other relationship, friendship with God requires good communication—good *two-way* communication. We know that He listens when we talk to Him. But if He's talking to us and we don't know how to listen, communication won't occur and relationship with Him will be affected.

In the first three lessons, we talked about the fact that prayer is a dynamic relationship. This week, we're going to explore what it means that relational prayer is conversational. Our prayer lives will be transformed when we understand that God is talkative and wants to engage us in two-way communication.

About now you may be sputtering, "Yeah, but . . ." You may have doubts, questions, objections, or reservations. If so, don't worry. For many of us, the idea of God communicating outside the pages of Scripture or the majesty of creation is a new and challenging thought. Most of us haven't experienced such two-way conversation with Him. But receiving direct communication from God is where the relationship with Him becomes most real and tangible.

2. When you think of God communicating with you, what do you feel comfortable with? Uncomfortable?

3. Read the following verses and underline whatever you see that suggests communication from God to His people or from His people to God.

> My heart has heard you say, "Come and talk with me."
>   And my heart responds, "LORD, I am coming." (Psalm 27:8, NLT)

> I listen carefully to what God the LORD is saying,
>   for he speaks peace to his faithful people. (Psalm 85:8, NLT)

> Come, all you who are thirsty,
>   come to the waters;

and you who have no money,
   come, buy and eat!
Come, buy wine and milk
   without money and without cost.
Why spend money on what is not bread,
   and your labor on what does not satisfy?
Listen, listen to me, and eat what is good,
   and your soul will delight in the richest of fare.
Give ear and come to me;
   hear me, that your soul may live.
I will make an everlasting covenant with you,
   my faithful love promised to David. (Isaiah 55:1-3)

Call to me and I will answer you and tell you great and unsearchable things you do not know. (Jeremiah 33:3)

I will climb up to my watchtower
   and stand at my guardpost.
There I will wait to see what the Lord says
   and how he will answer. (Habakkuk 2:1, NLT)

My sheep listen to my voice; I know them, and they follow me. (John 10:27)

The Spirit himself testifies with our spirit that we are God's children. (Romans 8:16)

If any of you lacks wisdom, he should ask God, who gives generously to all without finding fault, and it will be given to him. But when he asks, he must believe and not doubt, because he who doubts is like a wave of the sea, blown and tossed by the wind. (James 1:5-6)

For further study, go to www.navpress.com/pray/content .aspx?id=4352, where you'll find the article "God Is Not Silent," which will give you more scriptures about God's communication with us.

4. According to these passages, what are some of the benefits of hearing from God personally?

    a. Can you think of additional ways someone could benefit from hearing from God personally?

    b. Do any of these benefits appeal to you? Which ones?

5. According to these passages, does the listener have to do something to invite God's communication? If so, what?

When I was struggling with my husband's illness a few years ago, a friend asked me if I was hearing from God. I thought about different questions I'd posed to God (I usually wrote them in my journal). Many times I'd reflect back a week or two later and realize I'd discovered God's answer as I read Scripture, heard a sermon, saw events unfold, or found peace in my heart where there'd previously been discord.

So I told my friend, "Yes, I hear from God."

He pressed. "How often do you hear from God, would you say?"

"How often?" His persistence surprised me.

"Yes, how often? Like, for example, what did He say to you this morning?"

Well, I hadn't heard anything from God that morning. So I ignored that question and decided to try to quantify how often I heard from God. "I'd say I hear from Him about 25 percent of the time when I ask Him something." Obviously I was just guessing.

"I feel sorry for you!" he exclaimed, noticeably sad that I heard from God so rarely. Then, gently, he assured me that God had much to say to me in the middle of my perplexing and painful situation if only I would take time to listen.

My friend's suggestion sent my heart and mind racing with questions, doubts, longings, and hesitations: Was the God of the universe really willing to speak personally into my life circumstances? How would I know if it were really God speaking and not my wishful thinking? What if God asked me to do something I didn't want to do? What if the enemy hijacked the conversation? Did I have time for a two-way conversation with God? Relationships take time! Yet, wouldn't I experience God's love and presence more if He were to talk to me?

Finally, I decided that the pros outweighed the cons. If God were truly willing to speak to me—which I had to admit seemed to be what Scripture said—then I would find the time, make the effort, take the risk, and invite Him to do it.

Hearing from God didn't happen overnight nor did all of my questions instantly evaporate. But I want you to know this: Inviting God to teach me to hear Him has been the best thing I have ever done for my prayer life. In fact, it's been one of the best decisions I've made for my life in general. Nothing has transformed my life with God, my enjoyment of Him, my willingness to follow Him, and my confidence and trust in Him more than learning to hear His personal words to me.

6. How do you react to my story? Do you share any of my questions? Perhaps you have questions of your own. Jot down your reactions and questions.

7. Suppose God were to speak to you—not just on rare and dramatic occasions, such as when He spoke to Moses from the burning bush, but regularly and in everyday life. What if, for example, you were to pray, "Lord, I'm discouraged and sure could use some hope here," and He were actually to reply? Or if you said, "I'm so grateful for who You are and what You've done for me," and He said, "Would you like to know how it makes Me feel to hear you say that?" Or if you were to say, "I really don't know how to handle this difficulty in my family right now," and He answered, "I have some ideas. Want to hear them?"

Think about some of the things on your heart and mind right now. Imagine that instead of just sending up a one-way prayer, you were able to engage God in a two-way conversation. There would probably be some excitement and anticipation for you, but you might also feel intimidation and reluctance. What would the pros and cons be if prayer actually were a two-way dialogue instead of a one-way monologue? List every positive and negative you can think of.

Positives   **Negatives**

If you aren't accustomed to hearing personally from God, you may have many questions—more than I can answer now. For the moment, I'd like you to grapple with the idea that left my head spinning: Maybe there is more—much more—to prayer than we've known, and our talks with God might change radically if we are willing to embrace the idea that God communicates personally.

TALK IT OVER

PRAYER RESPONSE: EARS TO HEAR?

1. Go back to question 7 and pick the positive or negative that most strongly describes what you think or feel about hearing from God personally at this stage of your spiritual journey. Write it here, and then

tell God your honest thoughts and feelings about it, whether they seem acceptable to you or not. Record the first sentences of what you tell Him.

2. Based on what you know about God's Word and His character, listen for how you think God is responding to what you just shared with Him. Tell Him that you want to hear from Him alone and no one else—not even your own thoughts; then trust Him to guard and direct what you hear. Does He give you a scripture, picture, thought, or memory? Write down the response you sense He may be giving you.

> **TALKING POINTS**
>
> Remember to practice the key prayer ideas we've discussed so far:
>
> 1. Prayer is relational, so talk to God as you would to a friend.
>
> 2. Risk talking openly and honestly about what you feel and think.
>
> 3. Upgrade your view of God by talking to Him according to His true character.
>
> 4. God wants to engage us in two-way communication, so allow space for it.

3. If you sense He is saying something to you, even if it's just a vague impression at this point, respond to what you think He might have said. Keep the conversation going. Summarize the main points below.

CONTINUE TO PRACTICE

Which of the following prayers fits you best right now?

- ☐ "God, I kind of doubt You would speak to me. But if I'm wrong, would You please show me? I don't want to miss out if this is something You have for me."
- ☐ "God, I thought You only spoke to people in Bible times. I really didn't think You would speak personally now, but I'm willing to have You show me otherwise. If You really do speak today, would You help me to see it from Your Word as well as from any other source You use to reveal it to me?"
- ☐ "I'm ready, God. I want to hear from You personally. Please teach me how to hear and know Your voice. Speak, Lord, I am listening" (see 1 Samuel 3:10).

☐ Write your own prayer here:

Pray the prayer you selected every day for the rest of this week (or longer, as desired). Listen and watch for what God might say to you in response. Pay attention to thoughts that enter your mind, passages you read in Scripture, songs that pop into your head, messages you hear in church, Bible study, or Christian media—and anything else that might be God seeking to get your attention. Record any response you sense He might be giving you.

Notes About Your Experience:

TUNING IN TO GOD'S EVERYDAY VOICE

KEY IDEA:

If we're to relate with God in two-way relationship, we need to become aware of the different ways He speaks and learn to discern His voice.

I ADMIT IT. I balk at many of the newer forms of communication technology. I got my first cell phone nearly a decade after many of my friends had theirs. Even then, I didn't text with it. Recently a good friend was surprised I hadn't responded to the news of her mother-in-law's death. Horrified, I said, "But I didn't know!"

> **SUGGESTIONS FOR PACING THE LESSON**
>
> Days 1–3: Work through "Consider This" at the beginning of the lesson.
>   Days 4–7: Do the prayer exercises in "Talk It Over" and "Continue to Practice."

"Didn't you get my text?" she replied.

I hadn't. As a result, I wasn't able to support my friend during her time of loss.

I have other friends who avoid the phone, or their voice mail. One time I needed to set up a rehearsal with a fellow violin player. I called all three of her phone numbers and left multiple messages, but I got no response. I tried for many days with no success. I was communicating, but she wasn't hearing me.

CONSIDER THIS

1. I mentioned just two methods of communication in the previous examples; the means we have to communicate seem to be endless!

    a. Following are just a few methods of communication. Check any that you use but one or more of your friends don't use.

        ☐ Facebook, Twitter, or other avenues of social media
        ☐ Handwritten letters, birthday cards, and thank-you notes
        ☐ Doing things together
        ☐ Acts of kindness or service
        ☐ Long face-to-face conversations
        ☐ E-mail
        ☐ Phone calls

    b. How does the fact that one of you likes to communicate a certain way and the other doesn't affect your relationship?

For a long time I had a similar communication disconnect with God. I was limited in the ways I allowed Him to communicate with me. He could speak to me through His Word, through people (especially preachers or Christian musicians and authors), and perhaps through circumstances—but that was about it. I either wasn't aware of or was skeptical of other modes of communication.

I've talked with many Christians who can relate to my experience. But I've also learned that if we're to relate with God in two-way relationship, we need to become aware of the different ways He speaks and learn to discern His voice.

2. What are God's methods of communicating? To answer that question, we need to look at scriptural examples. Many times, passages will tell us that God communicated, but they don't tell us the method used. For example, the Holy Spirit revealed to Simeon that he wouldn't die until he'd seen the Messiah, but we aren't told how that revelation happened (see Luke 2:26). Sometimes all we know is that "God said" or "the word of the Lord came." Other passages indicate the methods God uses. Look up the passages below and discover a means by which God spoke. Don't be worried if you find a little overlap among the sets of passages. Sometimes God combines methods!

   a. Matthew 17:1-8; Luke 3:21-22; Acts 9:1-7

   b. 2 Chronicles 36:22; Ezra 1:5

   c. 1 Kings 19:11-13

   d. Joel 2:28; Matthew 2:12

e. Acts 2:17; 10:9-16; 16:9

f. Luke 1:26-38; Acts 8:26; 27:21-25

g. Psalm 19:1-4

h. Numbers 11:25-26; 1 Samuel 19:20; Luke 1:67; Acts 19:6

i. Psalm 119:105; 2 Timothy 3:16-17

j. Amos 4:6-13

k. Romans 8:16

3. Which of these forms of communication does God use with you? Circle all that apply in question 2. If you don't think God speaks to you or if He speaks to you in other ways, write your thoughts here.

4. Along with being aware of *how* God communicates, we need to learn to tune in and discern *when* He's speaking to us. Here are three steps that will help us do that.

The first step is one I needed to do: Open up, invite, and expect God to speak. As I opened myself up to the possibility that God might want to interact with me in a consistent, close relationship, I started to see more biblical basis for that longing. From what I was learning through Scripture, hearing from God was the norm; hearing nothing was cause for concern.

That realization built my faith, which allowed me to expect Him to speak. Until then, I reasoned that if God wanted to say something to me, He was free to do so. Occasionally I'd invite Him to speak, but when I didn't hear anything right away, I figured He didn't want to talk to me and let myself slip back into doubting that an interactive relationship with Him was possible. It was a huge turning point when I decided I'd expect God to speak and keep asking Him until He either helped me hear or convinced me I wasn't supposed to.

    a. Have you ever invited God to speak to you? If so, what happened?

5. Along with inviting God to speak, we often need to identify barriers to being able to hear His voice.

    a. Check any of the following hindrances to hearing that might apply to you.

        ☐ Not taking time to listen
        ☐ Doubting He will really speak
        ☐ Not knowing what His voice sounds like
        ☐ Concern about replacing scriptural objectivity with subjective personal experience
        ☐ Misperceptions of God's character
        ☐ Unconfessed sin
        ☐ Distractions
        ☐ Self-reliance, independence
        ☐ Fear of what He might say
        ☐ Lack of desire
        ☐ Being afraid of hearing the wrong voice
        ☐ Other:

    In my journey toward hearing from God, I had to deal with many of these hindrances. Early on I figured that if God were to speak to me, it would be dramatic and obvious; I had no clue what His "still small voice" sounded like (1 Kings 19:12, NKJV). Furthermore, though I truly did want to hear Him, I was afraid I might also be opening myself up to deception. And those were just a couple of my barriers!

As I became aware of each obstacle, I would talk to God about it. I'd confess my reluctance and ask Him to show me His truth and His desires for me. One by one, the hindrances fell away. In the end, I decided the risks of not hearing, and consequently leaning on my own understanding, were greater than the risks of hearing.

b. Look at the hindrances you checked. Ask God how He would like you to address these. His answers might include:

- Pray with a friend and ask God to show the two of you where the hindrance is coming from and what to do about it. (When I'm "stuck" on something, I can often hear better with a mature, discerning friend who knows how to hear from God. Often God will send me to such a friend for help.)
- Confess any resistance you are responsible for (e.g., self-reliance, independence), ask His forgiveness, and ask Him to help you trust Him in that area.
- Ask Him to heal your emotions (or seek help from some-one who can do emotional healing prayer) for issues that might have emotional roots (e.g., fear of what He might say).
- Ask a friend who does hear from God well to talk with you about your hindrances.
- Other (God is creative!).

c. After you've prayed about this, write down how you sense God leading you. If He is asking you to take a next step, record your plans for how and when you will do so.

DEVELOPING DISCERNMENT

Remember that learning to recognize God's voice is a skill that takes time, practice, and intentionality. Don't be discouraged if sometimes you think you're not hearing anything or you might be hearing wrong. That's normal for most of us when we're getting started.

Discerning God's voice from all of the other voices in and around us (our own thoughts, the philosophy of the world, the desires of our flesh, the temptations of the Evil One) is a skill that God is eager to develop in us. He wants to talk to you. He wants you to hear His voice and receive His love, affirmation, guidance, instruction, perspectives, and companionship. He is invested in the process of helping you to know His voice.

Here are three simple things to keep in mind:

1. God wants you to hear His voice. He does not want you to be misled. He will protect you from hearing the wrong thing because His sheep know His voice (see John 10:27). And Jesus promised that the Holy Spirit will lead you into all truth (see John 16:13), so trust Him to do that for you. Make it a practice to let Him know you want to hear Him only. If you ask Him to protect you from hearing other input, including your

own logic and understanding, He can be trusted to provide that protection.

2. Scripture is always the measure for what we hear. God may tell us things that aren't discussed in Scripture, but He will not contradict Scripture. God's voice is always consistent, whether through the written pages of Scripture or His Spirit speaking in our hearts.

3. God will speak to us in a way that is consistent with His character. He is never condemning or harsh. He invites, leads, and woos; He doesn't force, drive, or push. He brings out the best in His children like a good Father does. When He corrects, He does so lovingly because He wants you to experience the peace and joy that come from walking in His ways. Conversations with God should leave you feeling hopeful rather than defeated, accepted rather than judged.

(For more indicators of what God's voice sounds like, review His characteristics on pages 49–50 in lesson 3, along with the fruit of His Spirit in Galatians 5:22-23 and the qualities of His wisdom found in James 3:17.)

---

6. Finally, when tuning in to God, it's important to be aware of the necessity to practice your listening skills. Hearing God won't happen automatically for most of us. Until we learn to discern His voice, we often miss what He's saying.

There are different ways to tune in. One of the most important ones is a process that has been embedded in many of the prayer responses you've done throughout the study:

- Be intentional. Ask God questions.
- Then stop. Be still for a few minutes. Listen. Pay attention to what is happening in your heart and mind.

- Jot down what you think you might be hearing.

You probably haven't noticed this process because I haven't pointed it out to you in a list like this. But maybe now that you see it, you're thinking, *Well, isn't that interesting. . . . That's exactly what we have been doing in many of the prayer portions.* If you continue to incorporate these steps when you talk to God, you will take significant strides toward hearing from Him.

What has happened for you as you've tried this process the past few weeks?

As I opened up, expected God to speak, and dealt with some of the hindrances, I actually did start to hear more from Him. His voice didn't come with dramatic burning-bush experiences; usually He just gave me a thought or perspective that I wouldn't have had on my own. And that encouraged me to listen more. I also realized He'd been speaking all along, but I either hadn't been listening or hadn't been aware of (or open to) the variety of ways He likes to communicate.

TALK IT OVER

PRAYER RESPONSE: "CAN WE TALK?"

1. Tell God how you feel about Him speaking to you personally and more often. Does the idea excite you? Scare you? Fill you with questions? Are you more open to some forms of communication (refer back to question 2 on pages 71–72) than others? Talk to Him about that, too. Write your first sentences here.

2. Now, based on what you know about God's Word and His character, listen for how you think He is responding to what you just shared. Tell Him you want to hear from Him and no one else—not even your own thoughts—and then trust Him to guard and direct what you hear.

> **TALKING POINTS**
>
> As you talk with God, remember to practice the foundational prayer ideas we've focused on.
>
> 1. Prayer is relational, so talk to God as you would to a friend.
>
> 2. Risk talking openly and honestly about what you feel and think.
>
> 3. Upgrade your view of God by talking to Him according to His true character.
>
> 4. God wants to engage us in two-way communication, so allow space for it.
>
> 5. Be open to the ways God speaks and practice discerning His voice.

Does He give you a scripture, picture, thought, or memory? Remind you of a dream? Direct your gaze to something in creation? Fill you with deep inner peace and "rightness"? Write down the response you sense He may be giving you.

CONTINUE TO PRACTICE

Review the three steps in questions 4, 5, and 6. Where do you sense yourself in the tuning-in process? Which area do you need to focus on?

- ☐ Opening up, inviting, and expecting God to speak
- ☐ Dealing with barriers
- ☐ Practicing your listening skills

Each day, talk to God about the area you identified. Expect Him to help you and move you forward. He may ask you questions; listen and respond if He does. He might nudge you to study an idea in Scripture, talk to someone, or try something new in your prayer time. If He does, do it!

He will probably speak to you throughout the day about your area of focus. Keep in mind the variety of ways He speaks so that you don't miss Him. Plan time at the end of each day to review what He has said.

Write your thoughts, challenges, experiences, questions, and aha moments on the next page.

Notes About Your Experience:

KEEPING COMPANY WITH GOD

KEY IDEA:

Praying without ceasing comes naturally when we bring God into the everyday events of our lives and talk to Him about them along the way.

CONSIDER THIS

1. What does 1 Thessalonians 5:17 tell you to do?

a. If you had to describe to someone what that command means without using the word *pray*, what would you say?

> **SUGGESTIONS FOR PACING THE LESSON**
>
> Days 1–3: Work your way through the "Consider This" section.
>
> Days 4–6: Do the prayer exercises in "Talk It Over."
>
> Day 7: Begin one of the "Continue to Practice" ideas.

b. How does the thought of praying continually make you feel?

Praying continually is quite an order if we think God expects us to engage in nonstop intercession. Even half an hour of continual request-making would wear out most people. But what if this relational God who calls us His friends is asking us simply to keep company with Him? What if He wants us to include Him in every part of our lives and every part of our days? If we were to do that—to "practice the presence of God," as seventeenth-century French monk Brother Lawrence put it—talking with Him would become a satisfying, life-giving, energizing pursuit. This week we're going to discover that praying without ceasing comes naturally when we bring God into the everyday events of our lives and talk to Him about them along the way.

2. Look up Proverbs 3:5-6 and write the verses here:

3. Underline the phrases in the passage that call you to live in communion with God.

4. In our first week together, we considered Jesus' words in John 15, where He talked with His disciples about a friendship relationship with

them. In the portion of John 15 below, circle phrases that point to a moment-by-moment life with Him.

Remain in me, and I will remain in you. . . .

Yes, I am the vine; you are the branches. Those who remain in me, and I in them, will produce much fruit. For apart from me you can do nothing. Anyone who does not remain in me is thrown away like a useless branch and withers. Such branches are gathered into a pile to be burned. But if you remain in me and my words remain in you, you may ask for anything you want, and it will be granted! When you produce much fruit, you are my true disciples. This brings great glory to my Father.

I have loved you even as the Father has loved me. Remain in my love. When you obey my commandments, you remain in my love, just as I obey my Father's commandments and remain in his love. I have told you these things so that you will be filled with my joy. Yes, your joy will overflow! This is my commandment: Love each other in the same way I have loved you. There is no greater love than to lay down one's life for one's friends. You are my friends if you do what I command. I no longer call you slaves, because a master doesn't confide in his slaves. Now you are my friends, since I have told you everything the Father told me. You didn't choose me. I chose you. I appointed you to go and produce lasting fruit, so that the Father will give you whatever you ask for, using my name. This is my command: Love each other. (John 15:4-17, NLT)

5. Looking at the Proverbs 3 and John 15 passages together, how would you sum up your part in a moment-by-moment relationship with God?

6. Read Psalm 139:1-18. Using this passage as a foundation, imagine that God wanted to express His part in relating with you moment-by-moment. Write what you think He might say to you here. I've given you a start.

My friend, I already know you thoroughly. I am familiar with all your ways. . . .

TALK IT OVER

There are three prayer responses in this final lesson's "Talk It Over." I suggest doing one each day for three days.

PRAYER RESPONSE 1:
GOD IN YOUR ROUTINE

In the Proverbs 3 and John 15 passages you studied this week, you learned that God commands us to abide with Him and commit all of our ways to Him. But there's an exciting flip side to that equation: *God* is constantly abiding with *us*. Think about that! As we attempt to orient our lives to live constantly in His presence, we find He has already oriented His life to live with us. Let's take a look at what living with an awareness of this daily communion might look like.

> **TALKING POINTS**
>
> As you enjoy interacting with God through these prayer responses, remember to practice the foundational prayer practices we've learned:
>
>   1. Prayer is relational, so talk to God as you would to a friend.
>
>   2. Risk talking openly and honestly about what you feel and think.
>
>   3. Upgrade your view of God by talking to Him according to His true character.
>
>   4. God wants to engage us in two-way communication, so allow space for it.
>
>   5. Be open to the ways God speaks and practice discerning His voice.
>
>   6. Bring God into everyday events and talk with Him along the way.

1. List three routine things on your to-do list for today.

2. Now list three more routine things that are on your to-do list for the rest of the week.

3. If you tend to do these tasks while leaning on your own understanding, confess that to God now. What do you sense Him saying to you about that? Write it down here.

4. Ask Jesus to show you what it would mean to acknowledge and lean on Him, even to talk with Him as a friend, in one or more of the routine tasks you listed. What might the two of you talk about? Would you tell Him about your challenges and disappointments? Would you spend any time in side-by-side silence? How would His constant presence make you feel? How would your talks with Him throughout the day be similar to or different from what you usually think of as prayer?

Listen for His answer, and then record what you sense He might be saying to you.

PRAYER RESPONSE 2: "WHAT I LIKE ABOUT TALKING WITH YOU ..."

In this study we have explored five key ideas that are foundational to transforming prayer into a dynamic conversation with our relational God.

1. Put a check mark by the concept that has been especially meaningful for you.

    ☐ Lesson 1: Prayer thrives in the context of an authentic, dynamic, reciprocating friendship with God.

    ☐ Lesson 2: Your relationship with God deepens when you risk being open and honest with what you say to Him in prayer.

    ☐ Lesson 3: An accurate view of God fosters freedom and confidence in prayer.

    ☐ Lesson 4: God is talkative and wants to engage you in two-way conversation.

    ☐ Lesson 5: Learning to discern God's voice is essential to two-way relationship with Him.

2. Consider the potential the concept you marked has for helping you keep company with God. Make notes about how applying this principle could affect:

- How often you talk to God

- The content of your conversations with Him

- Your motivation to talk with Him

- Your enjoyment of prayer

- The way you pray with others

3. In view of your responses just now, write a prayer to God about what you are grateful for in your deepening friendship with Him, your hopes for conversations with Him in days to come, and what you need from Him in order to fulfill your part in cultivating your relationship.

For many years, I prayed primarily at set times: morning quiet times, before meals, with my husband before bed, and with fellow church members at services and functions. I rarely talked to God spontaneously, and I did not include Him in much of my ordinary life. Sure, I remembered to bring the "big things" to Him, but the little daily stuff? I pretty much handled it on my own. It never occurred to me that I could talk to God about it.

Since coming to understand some of the concepts I've shared with you in these lessons, my prayer life—and consequently my everyday relationship with God—has become more vibrant, exciting, and satis-fying. Here are just a couple of examples:

- Knowing God wants a reciprocating friendship with me encourages me to take all kinds of things to Him and to depend on Him for support. For instance, yesterday I had to make a phone call to someone who is going through a hard time and who is bristly as a result. Before I picked up the phone, I asked God for His input. I sensed Him steering me toward a specific focus and away from things I might ordinarily say. The phone call went unusually well, and knowing God was present with me as I made the call comforted me too.
- Because I know God wants to engage in two-way dialogue, I'm learning to pay attention to the thoughts that cross my mind so I don't miss conversations He wants to initiate. Just this morning while I was brushing my teeth before heading to a ministry-team meeting, the names of three people on the team popped into my head. In the past I would have dismissed it as a random, irrelevant thought. But today I asked God if there was anything He wanted me to know about these people. As we interacted, I heard more details about a specific need they had. So I asked God for confirmation: "If this is really You, would You please bring up the need at our meeting?" He did—through another person. I knew I was supposed to share and follow through on what He'd said to me earlier. It was exciting to be included in His plan for caring for the folks whose names He brought to mind. I love having Him talk to me!

For most people, connecting with God in dynamic, relational conversation is a process—usually a lifelong journey. Don't expect to jump from brief prayers of intercession to constant conversation with God (I'm certainly not there!). You will most likely experience a grad-ual deepening of your relationship as new discoveries and joys are added slowly but surely along the way. Celebrate each deepening of your connection with God, knowing that He is celebrating too!

PRAYER RESPONSE 3: "GOD, WHAT'S ON YOUR HEART?"

In this lesson we've been focusing on what it would be like to invite God into more of our days. But as you've been learning, relationship with God is reciprocal. He has thoughts and feelings about the way your relationship is growing, too. Finish this study by asking God to share His heart about *you*. One of the following questions may help you get started:

- "God, how do You feel about me inviting You into more of my everyday life?"
- "Father, what parts of my day have You especially been hoping to be included in? Why?"
- "Jesus, how do You see our friendship changing as I intentionally include You and talk to You more?"

Summarize what He says to you here, and then write your response to Him.

CONTINUE TO PRACTICE

I thought about calling this section "Practice the Rest of Your Life."
And truly, I hope that's what these prayer suggestions will end up being
for you. To get you started, consider what you have learned about
prayer in this study. Then read the ideas below and select one or two
you would like to incorporate into your daily life.

- ☐ As you begin your day, talk to God about what you think it will
  hold. What do you look forward to? What do you think will be
  hard or uncomfortable? Where do you especially need His help
  or encouragement? Ask Him to remind you to check in with
  Him as each of these things comes up during the day, and
  during the unanticipated events as well.
- ☐ When you read your Bible, expect God to speak to you personally. Listen for His words of personalized encouragement and
  affirmation or for fresh discoveries of what He is like and how
  He wants to relate to you.
- ☐ Picture Jesus with you at your job, home, or wherever you spend
  most of your day. Think about how close He is and how He
  wants to help, guide, and encourage you—and just be near you
  because He loves you.
- ☐ Ask God for help at the beginning of projects and undertakings
  throughout the day, whether large or small.
- ☐ Talk to God while you're driving or walking. Tell Him what you
  see; include Him in what you are thinking about.
- ☐ Pay attention to the random thoughts that pass through your
  mind. The song, person, idea, word, Scripture verse, affirmation, or warning that comes to you may be God speaking and
  inviting your response.
- ☐ When you are praying for someone or something, be sure to
  interrupt yourself and ask God what He'd like for that person or
  situation.

☐ If you mess up, tell Jesus about it right away. Know that He understands and forgives you. Picture Him looking into your eyes with love, forgiveness, and acceptance.

☐ When you see something beautiful or experience something that fills you with joy, express your delight to Him.

☐ Brainstorm with God. When you need wise and creative ideas, tell Him your question or challenge, and then take a sheet of paper and write down what comes to mind.

☐ Ask God to help you become more aware of your emotions. When you are feeling anxious, fearful, distressed, confused, embarrassed, upset, or lonely or when you experience some other uncomfortable feeling, share your heart with Him and ask Him to tangibly meet and care for you.

☐ When you are with other people, consciously remember that God is there too. As you interact with others, also listen to God and invite Him to help you know what to do and say.

☐ Before bed, review your day with God. Tell Him what was enjoyable and satisfying, as well as what was hard or discouraging. Consider how He might respond to what you share.

At the end of each day, reflect on where you and God kept company that day. You may want to write these in a journal so you can watch how your relationship deepens and develops in the days and weeks to come. Talk to God about what you did together that day and express your desires for the way you'll practice His presence tomorrow.

Notes About Your Experience:

AFTERWORD

I SORT OF ENVY God right now because He can sit down and have a chat with you about your experience with this study and I can't. I'd love to hear all about it and be there to affirm you for how you've opened yourself up to God in new ways and encourage you in the areas where you still want to grow.

Even though I can't sit and chat with you, I can anticipate what you might say: "I just got my feet wet, and it's over already." Or "I still have so many questions!" Or "I love what's happened between God and me these past few weeks, but I'm afraid it might stop without the study."

Am I close?

In some ways, sharing all these big ideas with you in just six weeks feels unfair. The concepts in this study took me years to practice and learn, and I'm *still* practicing and learning! I don't want you to think something is wrong if you're not where you'd like to be in your conversations with God.

If anything I'm saying is resonating with you, I have several suggestions that might encourage you as you continue on this journey.

- This one you could predict by now: Tell God how you feel. Let Him know what you're glad about with regard to the ways your relationship has grown, and tell Him where you are still hoping for more. Then listen — and keep listening in days to come — for His response. He will guide you.

- Continue using the "Talk It Over" and "Continue to Practice" prayer exercises. Make them a regular part of your prayer life. Remember that you learn to pray by praying.
- Find someone to join you on your journey of developing your relationship with God through prayer. You might ask someone who did this study with you, your spouse, or a close friend. Share your experiences with each other, including anything that is challenging or confusing. Pray with and for each other and be a sounding board as you each try to discern what you think you might be hearing from God.
- Do this study with someone else. Perhaps you'd like to start a group of your own and lead others through it. You'll get even more from it the second time around, especially if you're facilitating.
- Look for more studies in the BREAKTHROUGH PRAYER: STUDIES FOR SMALL GROUPS series by NavPress/*Pray!*
- Attend one of the "Deeper" prayer retreats I lead in Colorado Springs (visit www.gleneyrie.org and click on "Spiritual Retreats") or check into having me lead a retreat at your church (visit www.praymag.com and select *Pray!* prayer retreats).

I'm asking God to help you continue to deepen your connection with Him through prayer. And because He wants this far more than I do—and I want it pretty badly—I know He will do it!

ACKNOWLEDGMENTS

I ADMIT I WAS taken aback when a *Pray!* author I'd not even met in person had the boldness to quiz me about the frequency with which I heard from God and the nature of what I heard. But that surprising phone conversation (see story on pages 62–63) was what God used to forever change the way I view prayer and my relationship with Him. During the months that followed that phone call, Buddy Westbrook, who has become a close friend, patiently shared with me many of the principles I now share with you in this study. I will always be grateful to God for introducing me to Buddy and to Buddy for the generous ways he shares his life with me.

God has also blessed me with a most rare gift: an editor who is as passionate about the ideas I share in this study as I am. I implicitly trust Connie Willems with the editing of this study, not only because she is an outstanding editor but even more importantly because she is a genuine friend of God who talks with Him—and hears from Him—about everything, including my manuscripts.

Finally, I am most grateful to the sixteen small groups and their leaders who volunteered to pilot this study for *Pray!* and NavPress. They came from all over the country and represented all ages (eighteen to eighty!), several ethnicities, many denominations, and both genders. Each week they were guinea pigs for these studies—doing the homework, meeting together to discuss what they were learning, and giving us feedback on what worked and what didn't. Connie and I took their comments and suggestions very seriously. The study you have in your hands is much improved because of their contributions.

ABOUT THE AUTHOR

CYNTHIA HYLE BEZEK is a senior editor at NavPress, overseeing the *Pray!* enterprise of prayer resources for individuals and churches. She was editor of *Pray!* magazine until it ceased publication in 2009. She is a member of the National Prayer Committee; a prayer retreat leader who is passionate about helping people hear from God in relational, conversational prayer; and part of the leadership team for her local church's prayer ministry. Cynthia is the author of *Come Away with Me:* Pray! *Magazine's Guide to Prayer Retreats.*

This study is the first in the series of her new BREAKTHROUGH PRAYER: STUDIES FOR SMALL GROUPS prayer curriculum for small groups and churches based on the approach and philosophy of *Pray!* magazine.

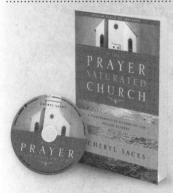

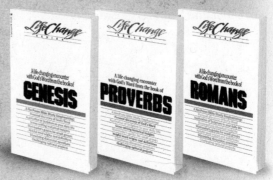

GLEN EYRIE

Glen Eyrie Spiritual Retreats

Glen Eyrie offers an ongoing lineup of retreats for Men, Women, Couples, and Ministry Leaders. Our desire is for these retreats to strengthen the foundations of your faith and to cause you to go deeper in your relationship with God!

Please visit our website for information on different spiritual retreats you can attend, dates, costs, and availability.

www.gleneyrie.org/retreats

GLEN EYRIE
Christian Camps and Conferences

SUPPORT THE MINISTRY OF THE NAVIGATORS

The Navigators' calling is to advance the gospel of Jesus and His kingdom into the nations through spiritual generations of laborers living and discipling among the lost.

Navigators have invested their lives in people for more than 75 years, coming alongside them life on life to help them passionately know Christ and to make Him known.

The U.S. Navigators' ministry touches lives in varied settings, including college campuses, military bases, downtown offices, urban neighborhoods, prisons, and youth camps.

Dedicated to helping people navigate spiritually, The Navigators aims to make a permanent difference in the lives of people around the world. The Navigators helps its communities of friends to follow Christ passionately and equip them effectively to go out and do the same.

To learn more about donating to The Navigators' ministry, go to **www.navigators.org/us/support** or call toll-free at **1-866-568-7827**.

THE NAVIGATORS®